CW00402361

WRISTWATCH

JAY WHITTAKER

Jay Whittaker

Iona 2019

INDEPENDENT INNOVATIVE INTERNATIONAL

Published by Cinnamon Press
Meirion House
Tanygrisiau
Blaenau Ffestiniog
Gwynedd
LL41 3SU
www.cinnamonpress.com

The right of Jay Whittaker to be identified as author of this work has been asserted by her in accordance with the Copyright, Designs and Patent Act, 1988. Copyright © 2017 Jay Whittaker.
ISBN:978-1-910836-80-4

British Library Cataloguing in Publication DataA CIP record for this book can be obtained from the British Library.

Designed and typeset in Palatino by Cinnamon PressPrinted in Poland.

Original cover design by Adam Craig.

Cinnamon Press is represented in the UK by Inpress Ltd and in Wales by the Welsh Books Council.

Acknowledgements

Earlier versions of some of these poems have been previously published: 'Canopy' on the websites of the Cinnamon Press and Second Light Live; 'Risky breasts' on the Scottish Poetry Library website to coincide with the launch of the second edition of *Tools of the Trade: Poems for new doctors* in June 2016; 'Library of stones' in *Envoi 173*, July 2016; 'Pink snow' in *The Frogmore Papers 88*, September 2016; 'Guidewire insertion, pre-surgery' was longlisted for the 2015 *Mslexia* poetry competition and published, alongside 'Baited', in *Orbis 177*, November 2016; 'Carapace' was longlisted for the Fish Poetry Prize 2016 and shortlisted for the Bridport Poetry Prize 2016; 'Path' was published in *Brittle Star 39*, December 2016; 'Call and response' in *Far Off Places*, Summer 2017; 'Thank you, Vera' in *The Interpreters' House 64*, January 2017; 'Bed fellow' in *Impossible Archetypes 1*, March 2017, and 'You are invited to the wedding of Rob and Nigel,' was recorded for, geolocated and published on the website of Echoes of the City, an Edinburgh City of Literature podwalk.

Thanks to Jan Fortune and all at Cinnamon Press, and to Jane McKie, Roselle Angwin and all I met on retreat in Iona; Flora Sinclair, Carol Christie, and Edinburgh's Other Writers. A number of these poems began in Poetry School exercises—thanks to Warsan Shire, Andrew Philips, Katrina Naomi, and Carrie Etter. Carolyn Dougill, who told me I should write a book—here it is! To my friends and family—heartfelt thanks. I would not be here without you.

Contents

Punctured World

Risky Breasts

Whittled, Weathered

*In memory of Morag Watson,
with love and thanks for the past
& dedicated to Marie O'Donnell,
with love and thanks for the future.*

Wristwatch

Punctured World

Path

I was rabbit
riddled with mixy
grey pelt pocked with death,
flank heavenward,
eye film cooling.

I was frond
wrenched from the sea bed
desiccating, twisting
into wizened serpent:
my root, a face.

I am cairn:
taking my place
in a congregation of flotsam,
all the whittled, weathered,
stacked anew.

The call

A moment to rest, at last
the day's visiting done.

Flick through a mag
with unseeing eyes.

There's calm in exhaustion, a break
between work and visiting hours,

glimmer of how life will be
when she recovers: oxygen tank

behind her chair, bed downstairs.
The phone rings. Two lives end.

Whelk shell

I took succour from the mollusc
curved into my hard edge, twisted
round to my spire's hollow.

My indweller washed out of me.
I joined an infinity of empty shells,
dashed against each other.

Now, I am the singular spiral
of my whorl, contours smoothing
in the ceaseless wash of tides.

The hum

Sometimes at night, the city sighs and creaks,
seeps through my open window.
Did I leave a radio on in another room?
An orchestra plays, *diminuendo* -
but it's only the wind conducting the city.

Wind plucks chain link; tyres
sweep and roll the ring road.
Beyond the flap of plastic sheets,
a train's glancing horn-chime,
the shy creak of roof, cooling.

Listen as the city wheezes,
exhaling through its teeth:
the pause where it stops breathing,
when all I hear is heart,
thudding, as I wait.

Bed fellow

With the whole bed to choose from
the dog clambers in, so close
I almost fall off the edge.

I move to what used to be my side,
that familiar view across pillows
from which I turned away,

just as I had to sit in her armchair,
occupy her space,
to not see the gap she left.

White china

Thank you for registering your wedding list with John Lewis.

In china and glassware we can't help a habitual sneer
at couples shuffling between stations, beatified
by halogen. Yet now we're part of it,
newly respectable: we join the devotions.
Dinner plate, sauce boat, espresso cup –
from a distance all white china looks the same.
The set I like is thick, each plate solid
as a round of shortbread. Your favourite
has an oval indent, each plate a blank staring eye.
I turn away. And wonder at us,
dissembling love's young dream, thinking,
we could actually have a matching set.
Table linen. A canteen!
I balance a spoon on my finger.
Why, in twelve years together, didn't we do this before?
Were we really only waiting for a law to be passed?

A fine and private place

So, at the vows,
you say at length
what she means to you.
Set it out fully,
as one of you will,
again, alone
in front of a coffin.

At the registrar's desk,
you're left to record
her parents' occupations,
dates. Filing her life
for historical record,
only you hold the data,
their soul keeper.

Pink snow

Every spring, cherry trees smirr
at their tips, buds swell
like alveoli till they burst.

My first April alone
in twenty years. I miss you
cursing pollen, reaching for Piriton.

After a storm, my private glee
in kicking blossom-fall—
no-one to keep secrets from any more.

Ladies' sightseer

After six months your estate is settled.
I pay off our mortgage. *Fifteen years early,*
the cashier smiles, *that must feel good.*
I can't explain. Your life insurance
as tainted as blood money.

Reeling along Rose Street, I look in shops,
anything to distract me, and in Tiso find
a pair you thought discontinued
brazen on the rack. Pristine
Ladies' Sightseer, size 6 (grey) —

the only shoes to fit your swollen
feet towards the end. Moulded to your toes,
insoles worn to nothing at the heel:
after you died, I couldn't face them any more.
I dropped them in the wheelie bin on my way to work.

Sea defence

She was sting and salt of sea on my lips;
a seal stranded on a causeway.
Knotty and fraught as a newly felled trunk,
and now, driftwood.

Taut, fraying guy rope;
she was a submerged cathedral.
A carved oak chest recovered from the depths,
motes of water, settling.

The life of stuff

Yes, I had a father. See his watch, his jigsaw,
the wooden toy fire engine he didn't finish.
Plastic ruler embossed *British Railways*, his Bible.

Yes, I had a mother. Spines peeling,
Marlborough-scented books fill forty crates,
and never the time or health to unpack them.

Yes, I was a daughter, girl-guide, pupil,
careful lettering on my brown-papered jotter:
Poppy Patrol songbook. 166th Glasgow.

Carried from home to home to storage unit,
each box a pepper-spray of past, emptied now,
folded flat, yes, for the crusher's claw.

Clearing unit A3021

The box of broken, worthless things:
your Mum's Scotland-shaped thimble holder
the pegs long since snapped off;
what I decided I couldn't sell—
18th and 21st birthday trinkets
(a faded pastel horseshoe, a plastic key)—
in yellowed, brittle cellophane.

Utility piece

It's time to rehome you,
Hippopotamus,
squat in the corner
scuffed veneer
the colour of the eighty a day
you absorbed for decades.

I never liked you.
I can say that now.
You came when I married
the youngest daughter.

No-one else had room for you
so we took you home,
fed you a terrible diet—
crammed you with board games
a tangle of connectors, adapters, chargers.

You belch booze-reek when I open your doors.

And now I'm widowed
I wonder why I tend you,
oxpecker-busy.
You were part of her childhood, not mine,
yet you've outstayed flat-pack and two sofas.

Oh Hippopotamus, handles chipped,
bulbous gnarly legs, too heavy to lift—
do you remember
after her funeral, in our home for the first time,
her brother said, outraged
How did YOU get that?

And I, the unhappy inheritor,
retold our story.

Singing bowl

Struck: the toll sets tissue, bone
quivering, fingertip to sole.

Losing track of sound, I set it down:
unheard reverb thrums the table.

Aeons may pass before we see
the speck of a dying star;

so each of us who ever breathed
may never stop ringing.

Oiseau

After Salvador Dali

Light leaches from the day. Not much caring about a way back through the dunes or when waves, lapping closer, will catch up. Uncanny sand, cold, each grain absorbs her. Skin cracks, sloughs. Her bones are not the shape she thought. She might have grown feathers from shoulder to elbow. But her skin kept her in.

Smashed open on the sand, ribcage a cist, cradling a shrivelled body, bulging eyes, legs mid-gallop: desiccated beyond naming.

O moon, you are hollow.

Risky Breasts

Risky breasts

Enjoy abseiling, hang gliding, roller coasters.
Are sloping off for a sly fag mid-morning.
Don't care what they eat: fish suppers,
pizza, doughnuts, Campbell's meatballs.
Will open that second bottle.
Are the bad girl in Grease, all surly attitude
leading to ruin. Don't care about their career,
spend six months in the Andes. Won't fasten their seatbelt
in the back, particularly not for short hops.
Spend up each month, never save,
always run petrol down to the fumes.
Jaywalking across junctions
in a country where traffic comes at you
on the other side to home.

Guidewire insertion, pre-surgery

The doctor didn't look like a Victorian entomologist
as she pushed her forearm, full weight
between my breasts
to be absolutely sure she would bore
into the lump
this time

I felt like a moth splayed in a case,
and no, technically, it didn't hurt
but oh the pressure, the puncture, the pinning.

Wide local excision

It's my turn to be the lone woman
staring at ripples on the canal.

Usually it's me, striding briskly past,
suspicious of anyone with time to kill.

Insulated against curiosity
the moment holds me:

delicate as a pond skater,
dappled sunlight on my face.

Elegy for biopsied sentinel nodes

Hold fast, sentinel nodes.
You kept me from danger
even while we slept.

Were you strong enough,
sentinel nodes?
Stained, dissected

on a slide,
my sacrificed sibyls—
tell me my fate.

Safety briefing

Please. No talk of journeys or battles.
One magpie flew at eye level,
parallel to the top deck.
All the buses coming at once
and never in threes.

Some measure the hours left.
Blessings, let's count them—
I'm standing, walking;
dear gods, stop me talking.
The number of hours stays the same.

Meanwhile, life crowds in:
at Tollcross, through the barber's window,
a cranium gleams. Even the bus
has advice for me, printed above the escape hatch.
You must leave all belongings behind.

You have no idea

Day 1, first chemo cycle

The nurse said, *I think I know the answer*
but is there any chance you're pregnant?
Oh no, I said (twenty years of playing this for laughs)
being a lesbian, I'd know.

I didn't want anyone there but you,
sent my mother away, imagined
you holding my hand as you would,
had you been there.

This will flush you out before we start,
said the nurse, *sharp scratch... well done.*
Cold saline snaked up my vein.
I tried to stay calm. It's supposed to help.

The nurse went to get the drugs,
came back empty-handed, said
The notes say your husband died last year,
that can't be right. You were very clear...

I said, *I ticked widow on your form.*
Cross out husband. Write wife instead.
Because she asked, I told her
all your hospital tales

and (because she asked)
how you died. She meant well.
That wasn't how I needed you then.
Another patient buzzed.

I'm so sorry, she said,
cast me
               adrift
                          in the chemo chair.

Canopy

Day 20, first chemo cycle

Do tree tips tingle, niggle like my scalp?
Most people's hair (I'm told) comes out on day eighteen.
White hairs worked loose first, waft down.
This late summer evening, my scarfed skull
as bald and vulnerable as a fledgling's,
I stand under the row of sycamore, my neck sore
from looking up to the abundance of leaves.
Whatever happens to me, the earth is turning.
At the same hour in winter, haven't I stood
in this very spot, watching bare branches
implore the sky for light?

Not-sleeping

Day 12, 2nd chemo cycle

4 a.m.
swims into sentience,
trawling murk, hinged maw agape.
Light-tipped siren stalk-baits swirling shoals, tangling fronds
to snag on rows of jagged, poised teeth.

Go no further

Floating poem

My bike grows furry:
dust clings to oil,
clogs the chain.

Energy precious,
I choose to walk outside,
not wash,

leaning against walls,
medic alert band as talisman
in case I can't speak.

Crumpled on a bench,
heart tolling,
I know the space between things.

All the near misses

Day 1, 5th chemo cycle

I lie on the trolley
floating, amniotic
after anaphylaxis.
Medics, monitors
banked around me
prove I live.

I can't cry for the dead.
I'm too busy crying
like a newborn, flayed
awake to a punctured world,
every breath outrage,
unable to stop breathing.

No one I love is near
to witness everything
has changed. No matter.
Only I am centre stage
at my birth, my death,
and all the near misses.

Baited

Day 10, 6th chemo cycle

I should have seen it coming. Narrow pavement, that pointer off-lead, trotting towards us, body-builder owner not really looking. My own dog, on-lead, over-protective, growling.

He turns, bellows. Fury sluices me, a shocking tonic. I tear off my wig, stuff it in his face, shouting, *You're angry? This is worth being angry about.*

When he has gone, I have to lean against a wall.

My favourite version. I often think about it, my lightning conductor.

Tamoxifen 20mg tablets

Take one daily for ten years.

500 of you down the hatch so far—
I pop you from green film,
oval crevice on one side
inscrutable as a cat's iris.

I no longer read your potential,
spelled out in miniscule print,
and folded into every box.
I know well what you do to me:

skin thins, cracks; the hot seethe
rises through me exactly like terror
of hospital ceilings, the doctor's serious face,
the box of tissues, the worn hessian chair.

Wristwatch

Day 365 after first chemo infusion

Twelve months since the first dose
cold-scorched up my arm
a vein at my wrist still bulges
slug-plump, keeping Kairos time.

Shriven by cytotoxins,
spring-heeled, today
I could vault the trees.
My dog pelts towards me,

effortless greyhound ecstasy,
looping, loosening,
and catching his joy, I sprint
because I can.

Annual check-up

The Pentlands have been wheeled closer.
Inigo Jones couldn't have devised a better fancy:
the sun picks out Caerketton's every crevice,
vivid grass ices Allermuir's softer slopes.

These hills are always there, in the gap
between church and trees, sometimes hazed
by cloud, haar, or my own distracted gaze.

Oblivion, Water of Leith

Through a half-open iron gate,
make for the river.

Something moves ahead, between trees,
avoiding me as a deer would.

The smell of weed brocades the air
and I see him—face as worn

as the washed rock, leather fedora,
denim faded grey: deliberately

not meeting my eye. I take pity—
he only wanted to get stoned

alone by the tumultuous roar,
watch the weir, the white falls

cutting between tenements,
the city's hidden vein.

I pick my way back
to the tarmacked path, think how,

if time were running out and I knew it,
better to get hammered, float face down.

An illustrated guide to the ruins

This bombed-out husk (established 1968),
roof sheared by the initial blast,
internal fittings razed by subsequent fire,
appears as derelict as a structure twice its age.
The shell remains serviceable.

Further excavations reveal pervasive rot
spreading through timbers.
An extensive course of damp proofing
reinstates the original look and feel,
but note: joists permanently weakened.

And of the future? The occupier,
once tempted to abandon to lichen,
ivy, has realised the space
(no longer fit for its former purpose)
has fabulous potential for parties.

Whittled, Weathered

Into the third year

I've counted
four birthdays,
two death days,
one cancer
since you died.

At Whitesands,
treading the liminal path,
the very point where the tide turns,
sand spread smooth
as though by a knife,

I remember what the undertaker said:
When scattering, turn
the urn upside-down
in a carrier-bag, cut
a hole in the bottom, walk.

Perhaps now it's time
for something else,
to throw you up in the air.
You'll settle on me
like dandelion clocks.

Reversioned

September: I catch
Richter's Recomposed Vivaldi
overlaying, chopping the familiar
saw and stir of the Four Seasons,

ornamented, live, beyond
my window by sparrows,
each time different
even on repeat.

This anniversary,
as much in my veins
as the well-kent chords,
dying back, creating something new.

1976

i

Arch back, flex arms: I arc and soar, the swing's swoop taking me higher than the town below.

Swing chains snap and jerk—*this time, no this time, no*—at full extent, links pull taut and pinch palms. As far out as I can—*this time*— I dive, a swallow's swoop to the scuffed brown earth.

ii

The sweet smell of metal on skin, a tang that survives soap, unlike the secret, singed smell in the crook of my arm from a day in the sun's scorch. I sniff my knees, my palms. Maybe no bath this week, either.

iii

Ours is the highest road on the hill. The town glints beneath me like a pile of crumpled Quality Street wrappers.

Crouching, I listen for the fire siren's blare. *The grown-ups tense at the air- raid klaxon on war films.* It's sounding six, seven times a night this summer—*someone's barn someone's house someone's bed*—calling firemen to the station. *Please don't let it be Gran or anyone I know.*

iv

The mains are almost dry. We are days away from standpipes. Each night I count more sirens, chill thrilled, from my watchful place on the edge.

Left to dry

I make a burrow from open, drying brollies.
The stiff-bristled rug abrades
my bare knees, elbows.
I am a water rat and I won't come out,

not for biscuits, certainly not for Gran,
thunderous above me. I wait,
curled into a ball.
With a crash, clatter, clap, she is gone.

Yes, I knew it would be terrible.
Yes, I am bad.
I crawl out to face Mum.
She'll never let us forget that.

Happy Christmas, 1978

Not expected: a glossy book
with satisfying new-paper tang,
The Human Body. I am ten
the year my parents gift me sex ed.

Respectable, published by M&S,
although it contains pages
of blood vessels, skeletons, brain,
what rivets me

(sitting amid ripped-off paper,
posh chocolates, tiger-feet slippers,
hoping no-one spots my interest)
is a diagram, cross-section: fucking.

Sleeping Beauty

The curse lifts, and Sleeping Beauty wakes
laid out in her own room. Her hands
wrinkled like her mother's.
A mirror shows wiry hairs,
chin bristles, a thirty year war
with girldom over.
But this is still her body.
Her mind still works.
This time round she knows
how she will inhabit her world, expand
to fill all her corners: it's dizzying,
a whole new tale. She's a crocus
punching up through sallow winter grass.

Conditional

After Sarah Kane

Yes   well   you wouldn't want them to think badly
         of us   you wouldn't want them to
                  oh I don't know
         strangers meddle   judge

no, better always to turn away
bite your lip   (no-one's looking)
                  (no-one must ever know)

what if someone we knew saw   what if—
someone we knew   found out

Is it safe?
we'll live opaque as chameleons, no-one will read us
                  —what if we—if—

Tree top, Melton Road

At eye level, the acer sighs,
heaves toward me, its tousled top
more lumbering beast than tree.

Sparrows dart, hop: synaptic
in gnarled, knuckled branches.

Cooling towers, Ratcliffe-on-Soar

From this flat Midlands plain,
stark vases funnel plumes,
billow sky-blots.

Careless in our cars, tutting
that such relics *burn Russian coal,*
just power them down,

or better yet, detonate.
Look to the canal, where Shire horses,
blinkered, once plodded.

Reinternment

Leicester, March 2015

A Midlands town reinvents itself,
breathes new meaning into an old death.
The echo of a gesture,
not where Richard lived or fell
but where he lay, under tarmac crust,
cars settling on top like eczema.

If a funeral's for those left behind
reinternment is a curious thing.
The line ends, and who's to remember?
Girl choristers sing;
an actor snubs the national anthem.
We outlive our own memories,

they slough from us like skins.

A home front

From behind the net I step back.
You glance up, sensing my gaze:
another living wraith, wrapping cardi
over shoulders. I want to haul up the sash,
hang the blackout tape, call as loud as the all-clear

I understand! I see people cross the street,
smile glassily through you, talk of anything
except the obvious lack of baby
since the doctor left your door, pale, head down,
carrying a bundle like a packet of fish.

I thought we'd get used to death
in wartime. Every broadcast
stuns us further, brothers, sons, husbands
slaughtered. We lurch at each rumour.
Hundreds dead in Coventry. Clydeside razed.

You won't have noticed in your smog of grief
no-one knows what to say to me either.
At least Martha's mother had the decency to write
—as next of kin, she got the telegram—
a woman friend, well, what does she matter?

You don't bother with the shelter now.
I don't go myself. I've had enough
of empty words: *so sorry for your trouble.*
Let's switch on lights, fling curtains wide,
draw down bombs to the ones who want to die.

The geologist's daughter

1

I struggle to name Lewisian gneiss
strewn across white sand,
ochre lichen shrouding
boulders with a fierce skin.

I never took the time to notice
(he never took the time to show me),
but we both are shaped by a love
of scrambling over rocks.

2

Whitley Bay, 1945. A miner's clever son
clambers over railings
against Mam's express command

to the swimming pool hewn from cliff:
names mudstone, siltstone,
limestone, sandstone.

3

Fast forward 65 years.
The house an empty limpet
I cleared and sold.

My father, landlocked,
if prompted remembers the foghorn
through a sea-fret of forgetting.

Reliquary

Battered black tin box, trim chipped,
key lost. Inside, shallow coin trays fold out
to reveal the compartment for notes and cheques.

I found it, empty, looking like nothing much,
but kept with birth, death, wedding certificates,
and chits whose ticks and copperplate scrawl

showed the mornings Grandma had been to school
and so, by law, could clock in
for an afternoon shift at the mill.

Vestige

I went out with some of the girls, she says.
There was a little boy in the bar. His Mam
had died, he was all upset. So I sang
a funny song to make him laugh.

It was kind to cheer him up,
I say, wondering,
did they go out?
They never go out.

We had a lovely trip, she says.
Me and some of the girls. Yesterday
… or last week I think …
Anyway someone must have died.
A few of us went for a party after.

A wake? I ask.
The room next to hers stripped
of cards and knick-knacks.
The mattress bare.

Eyes wet, she says, *They told me*
Mam's dead. Oh —
(I take her hand)
Can that be right?
Please tell me the truth.

Death hangs in the air

Thick as immanent rain.
The relief of downpour as tears
decongest nostrils.

The fragile, tender spot
in the pause between tears.

Rag trade

Afterwards
there is silence:
careful corralling of pins,
dusting fuzz from the looper.
This machine I tend,
spare time hobby:
two blades, two needles
four spools of thread
one head, foot,
pedal.

Fingers, girls!
Embroidery
machines punch logos on socks,
hammer wire wool in our heads,
clatter out any
college reading—
six spools, six needles,
twelve heads, two girls
one hand bar—
Fingers!

One summer's
work didn't kill me:
lint barely clung to my clothes.
By necessity, Grandma
made her living in the mill,
fuzzdust wadding lungs.
My wire brush echoes
her cushioned cough,
persistent
spittle.

Incantation (St Columba's Bay)

Anchor us now on this clacking,
rattling patchwork of rock!
A skirl of hail
is all that nails us to this world.

Quilt us, plait us into moss
knots of cast-off wool.
Hard for a woman to walk
trying to find her path, slantways,

stumbling.

Library of stones

The worst room to clean:
all those leather spines,
skin of ordinary beasts
embossed with letters I cannot read.

And not just words:
pictures—the lewdest sort.
the young master showed me,
tried to sit me on his lap,

then pushed me from him,
called me *harlot*,
said he would have me *let go*—
but he didn't even rise to that.

I pity him. I sort the linen;
I know whose breeches he stirs for.
The words we speak,
are they so different

from the ones in books?
Do they thunder
like the minister on Sunday?
The master, hoping to impress,

calls himself *a natural historian*,
counts rocks into footering piles:
glittering grey pebbles,
tiny tombstones,

one brute heavy as iron,
a long green vein through it.
Another called to me: mute red
no bigger than my palm

I slipped it in my apron,
lived for days in fear he'd miss it.
But he has so many. I am careful
to take from the bottom of the pile,

to keep only one. I am not a thief,
no more than he is.
They are not his because
he picked them up and labelled them.

Rock pool at Dun Í

Wind-flicks, glitterings,
dancing like mica.
One gust casts confetti
across the grey-brown pool.

Sometimes I know what I need
like a lamb diving for milk.

Beachcombed red epiphyte

I catch what I can.
Rigid tendrils
snag shattered shells,

my hold-fast a brittle
sand-gritted hinge,
stalk curved, hollowed.

I miss the sap
in every crimson thread.
Hefted by parasites

we are more than drift-twig,
whelk-eggs, kelp.
We are new, unnamed.

Call and response

Their chant, more desolate
than any song of the seas, seeped
through red stone walls to the water's edge,
drew me from tide to shingle.

I heaved myself onto rocks,
wanting more of their reedy keening,
and sang the song of the hermit crab.
A solitary woman spotted me, started

and ran, bare heels flashing.
She returned with a double
of the shroud she wore,
brown as wrack but dry,

chafing my shoulders raw.
There, she said, *you'll do*,
pressed one finger to my mouth.
I kissed it, my tail curling round her,

leaving marks the length of her gown.
When she fetched others
I sang their lament back to them.
Look at the Sister washed up, coracle lost.

She doesn't speak our tongue. Her voice!
They carried me to their tidy gardens,
so far from billows of kelp,
past the red stone wall

where the carved hag squats,
showing the cowrie between her legs.
In the cavernous room they call *chapel*
I sang with them the song I'd heard.

For that briefest time I knew
the intoxication of air—
till I sang the song of the hermit crab.
They threw me back to the sea

as they would mackerel, slapped
my weeping friend to silence.
Hooded figures turned away from me.

On rocks held apart by foam
I wait for the tide to swirl me back,
to breathe again the ocean.

Street furniture

Would you want your child to sleep rough tonight? Blue Comic Sans sign on the gate to a basement flat. Unhurried, a traffic warden consults the meter and strolls on, surveying parked cars. Not so many spaces to troll: it's a short street, its Georgian houses inscrutable, hard to tell whether respectable stone steps lead to mosque or flats. A few doors down, *Michele is a fat slag* scrawled in indelible ink beside the university swipe card reader. At this end of Roxburgh Street, the other blue plaque: *Peter Ware Higgs wrote the papers which predicted the Higgs Boson in this building in 1964.* Inside we are distracted by dogs barking, pock and rattle of car on cobbles, the universe unravelling.

You are invited to the wedding of Rob and Nigel

Outside the city chambers
summer rain dries on Old Town cobbles.
Tourists clamour round our hatinators, heels,
looking for a bride who never appears.

Instead, indulgent looks, double takes;
two young men ask to hug the grooms.
From the High Court, Hume (one moob showing),
looks on. St Giles is still amid the ebb.

We are a piece of history here, following
rainbow, Saltire flags to the reception.
Today the sun has broken through,
every summer morning different.

Possibility

The sun rises as it must every morning.

Slumbering still, the dog lifts his head,
and a roar of energy surges.
I could pump up tyres and cycle to work,
walk the dog up Wester Craiglockhart
to see how it looks today,
at this hour, in this moment.
Write letters to a far-off government,
march on an embassy. Work too,
I could do what I am paid for.
Sing, freewheeling,
down Middle Meadow Walk,
garlanded by birdsong.
Meet my lover, channel the current,
touching her is touching life itself.
Count stars as they circle the sky
with me or without me.

Sun cream

Glide over me, soak in,
leave your residue, slick
prophylactic against scorch.

I know to reapply you
when the sun's heavy hand
starts to smart.

Yes, I know what I should do:
take shelter, wear a hat—but I want
that warm caress on my arms.

Second weekend together

Her arbour, July: unimagined
abundance spills over—

crimson-fronded crocosmia
leaves as tall as me, waving lazily

as the breeze stirs it awake.
I follow her along the gravel path,

more used to scrub grass at the hill top
the wind at my back, pressing me to sky.

But these are new times,
needing new ways.

Nestled in the cleft of her garden, the fruit
of her former lover's work, I bring

the urgency of dog days,
leaf tips already turning brown.

Carapace

When you lie with your back to me
facing outward, your tender parts kept to yourself,
you are the sum of your disappointments.
Being human, I can't help but take it personally.

Then you turn to me,
the softness of your hand on my hip,
because I have in some way pleased you
or the world has offended you less.

The turn at Tomgarrow

It doesn't take much to miss the waymarker:
a crouching cottage, pinned in place by pines,
a few seasons from melting under lichen.

Beyond the outbuildings, taller than us,
a gnarled tangle of ripped-up roots—
a tree torn from the forest floor.

We walk its length, feet sinking into thickets
of vivid moss, air clotted with the threat of rain.
Any sense of path peters out.

Wandering further into the woods,
we have strayed from our limits.
Less than a year ago I could barely stand.

The old terrors rise: why did I think
I could manage this walk?
Who will find us? What if I can't go on?

Thank you, Vera

Not for raising
my lover,
but for teaching her
the knack of pissing
without removing pants—
my passport to pee
ferociously, frank
as a horse.

I learned
your legacy at 47,
was speechless
at the freedom:
no walk's now too long
for the mid-life woman walker,
no need to hold back
on bottled water.

Gratitude comes
easy, often—
behind a rock
at St Columba's Bay,
in Ravensheugh bushes—
your memorial
a sheela-na-gig
you never knew

whose urgent stream
fizzes in the sand.

What the hare knows

Me: ankle-deep in the burn
scanning the fence for gaps

while agitated cows bellow.
I see a hare: watching me,

huge, legs folded in tightest pre-spring.
At the centre of its wary eye,

a still pool, ancient knowledge:
sometimes it is better to bide.

There is only one goal. To live
and, at the right moment, flee.

Drag

After Conchita Wurst

Shot silk sack, emerald rust,
hangs centre stage, empty folds
once slinky, sewn close-fit
to precisely skim my curves.

Two decades on, a sliver of my former self,
the dress I sewed with meticulous care
becomes drag. I pinch in darts, pleat seams,
twirl, add fuck-me heels, stick-on beard,

the long wig bought when I had no hair,
worn for a laugh. And isn't that the point?

Notes

A fine and private place: Andrew Marvell, 'To his coy mistress' — *'the grave's a fine and private place, but none, I think, do there embrace.'*

Conditional: Sarah Kane, *4:48 Psychosis* (Methuen, 2001)

Call and response: one of Scotland's few sheela-na-gigs is to be found in Iona's ruined nunnery.

'Possibility': Audre Lorde, *A burst of light* (1988): *I Am Your Sister: Collected and Unpublished Writings of Audre Lorde*, edited by Rudolph P. Byrd, Johnetta Betsch Cole, and Beverly Guy-Sheftall. OUP, 2009. Used with kind permission.